The Shiny Penny

Mark L. Barry

GUIDING STAR
BOOKS

Send feedback to: feedback@theshinypenny.com

Published by Guiding Star Books, New London, CT USA

ISBN-13: 978-0692872949
ISBN-10: 0692872949

Library of Congress Control Number: 2017905671
Guiding Star Books, New London, CT USA

Mark L. Barry can be reached at the following address: mark@theshinypenny.com

Available from Amazon.com and other retail outlets.
Available on Kindle and other online stores.
www.TheShinyPenny.com

*For Princess Liv of Philadelphia
and Little Tess.*

A shiny new penny

rolled down the
sidewalk one day.

It rolled through one puddle

past two bicycle wheels

three rocks

four dirt piles

five hungry ants

six legs

seven flowers

and eight blades of grass.

Then the penny took
nine bounces

and landed inside
ten fingers.

And before you could
count to eleven …

the little penny was
shiny again!

Author **Mark L. Barry** brings his lovable Shiny Penny character to life in this entertaining counting book. Mark is hopeful that *The Shiny Penny* will encourage young children to value and respect all forms of money, including the penny. Too often, pennies are seen discarded on the sidewalk, instead of being saved, invested or spent wisely, gifted, or donated. This is unfortunate, as pennies play an important role throughout the world. Just think of all the charitable organizations – and associated lives – that benefit from donated pennies! So, let's keep our pennies off the sidewalk…and let's always be on the lookout for opportunities to put our shiny pennies to work! A graduate of the University of Connecticut School of Business, Mark earned a MA in Economics from Trinity College. He resides on the Connecticut shoreline with his high school sweetheart, two service-oriented daughters, and a feisty West Highland White Terrier named James Bond.

www.ingramcontent.com/pod-product-compliance
Lightning Source LLC
Chambersburg PA
CBHW041237040426

42445CB00004B/59